Investing Time for Maximum Return

Melody Mackenzie
and
Alec Mackenzie

American Media Publishing
4900 University Avenue
West Des Moines, Iowa 50266-6769
800-262-2557

Investing Time for Maximum Return

Melody Mackenzie and Alec Mackenzie
Copyright © 1995 by Alec Mackenzie's Time Tactics®

This publication is designed to provide accurate and authoritative information in regard to the subject matter covered. It is sold with the understanding that neither the author nor the publisher is engaged in rendering legal, accounting, or other professional service. If legal advice or other expert assistance is required, the services of a competent professional person should be sought.

Credits:

American Media Publishing:	Art Bauer
	Todd McDonald
Project Manager:	Leigh Lewis
Editor:	Spectrum Communication Services, Inc.
Designer:	Dawn McGarrahan

Published by American Media Inc., 4900 University Avenue, West Des Moines, IA 50266-6769
First Edition

Library of Congress Catalog Card Number 94-73037
Mackenzie, Melody and Mackenzie, Alec
Investing Time for Maximum Return

Printed in the United States of America
ISBN 1-884926-28-2

Introduction

You have exactly as much time as the most successful people in the world. If you want to achieve the same high levels of success as these winners, you must treat your own time as a precious resource to invest for maximum return.

Time is valuable capital. If you squander it, you will not develop your abilities, take advantage of opportunities, or carry out your commitments. What's more, you certainly will not make the most of your life.

An astonishing number of people, who carefully manage all of their other resources, are frustrated because time continues to slip through their fingers. What is really slipping away is their lives.

What you do with your time makes up your life.

When you make the commitment to choose what you do with your time, you take control of your life.

This book shows you how to do that. It provides a complete process for managing your most precious resource — TIME. It will give you a strategy to maximize the use of your time.

It will also help you develop another ingredient without which you cannot succeed in managing your time. That ingredient is commitment. You will gain commitment when you fully understand that there are only so many minutes in life. When they're gone, they're gone. When you commit to making the most of your time and your life, you can gain the satisfaction of having used your minutes to achieve personal and professional goals that are truly your own.

So these are the key words: **commitment, choice,** and **control.** Together, they are the *Time Tactics® Process.*If you don't make the commitment to choose what to do with your time, someone else will choose for you. You then lose control of your day and, eventually, your life.

But when you choose, you are in control. This book will show you how to choose to control your own life.

Happy living!

Mel Mackenzie
Alec Mackenzie

About the Authors

Melody Mackenzie

Melody Mackenzie is President of Alec Mackenzie's Time Tactics®, an international consultanting firm on time management. The company developed and distributes Time Tactics®, a planner/organizer used by many sales, management, and professional leaders around the world. With Alec Mackenzie, Mel coauthored "Managing Your Goals," a cassette program, and has presented the well-known *Making Time Productive* time management program in the United States, Canada, Mexico, and Australia for a broad range of clients.

Alec Mackenzie

For more than two decades, business executives and their support staffs in over 40 countries have attended Alec Mackenzie's seminars on time management, leadership, and the management process. Dr. Mackenzie's books include *The Time Trap,* a classic among business books which has sold over a million copies and has been translated into 12 languages, and *Time for Success: A Goal Getter's Strategy.* Among the more than 60 articles published by Alec is "The Management Process in 3-D," one of the most requested reprints in the history of the *Harvard Business Review.* He also has published cassette programs such as "Mackenzie on Time," "Time to Sell," and, with Melody Mackenzie, "Managing Your Goals."

Additional Resources

from American Media Incorporated

Other AMI How-to Series Books:

Assertiveness Skills
Customer Service Excellence
Documenting Discipline
Effective Teamwork
High Impact Presentations
The Human Touch Performance Appraisal
I Have To Fire Someone!
Interviewing: More Than a Gut Feeling
Making Change Work for You
Making Meetings Work
Managing Conflict at Work
Managing Stress
The New Supervisor: Skills for Success
Positive Mental Attitude in the Workplace
Self-Esteem: The Power to Be Your Best
Ten Tools for Quality

Videos Pertaining to the Subject of Time Management:

Time Trap II
Stress: You're In Control

Available from the Authors:
Time Tactics®, a Planner/Organizer
(518) 274-1090

Other Videos Available On These Subjects:
Americans with Disabilities Act • AIDS Awareness • Banking • Business Writing •
Change • Communication • Computer PC Training • Conflict Resolution •
Creative Problem Solving • Cultural Diversity • Customer Service • Empowerment •
Ethics • Family and Medical Leave Act • Healthcare Employee Training •
Healthcare Safety • Icebreaker • Interviewing • Listening Skills • Motivation •
Outplacement • Paradigms • Performance Appraisal • Professional Image • Quality •
Retail • Safety • Sales Training • Sexual Harassment • Stress • Substance Abuse •
Supervision • Teamwork • Telephone Skills • Time Management • And Many More!

To order additional American Media Incorporated resources,
call your Training Consultant at
(800) 262-2557

TABLE OF CONTENTS

Chapter One

Time Management 101

Chapter Two

The Role of Goals in Time Management

Chapter Three

Discovering Where Time Goes—
A Tool You Cannot Do Without

Chapter Four

Putting Yourself in Control–
Understanding and Handling Timewasters

Chapter Five

Your Personal Action Plan

Chapter Six

Advanced Time Tactics—
Putting It All Together

Answers to Chapter Reviews

Time Management 101

Chapter Objectives:

After you have read this chapter and have completed the interactive exercises, you should be able to:

- ☑ Explain why time management is crucial.
- ☑ Define time.
- ☑ Describe the characteristics of time.
- ☑ Understand the paradoxes of time.
- ☑ Describe the basic elements of the *Time Tactics® Process*.

Why Manage Time?

The answer is simple. Your time is your life. What you choose to do with each minute becomes your life.

By the end of every minute, hour, and year, your life has changed. What you do with your minutes and hours will determine whether your life has changed for better or for worse.

So the questions become, "How important is your life?" and "How important is your career?" If they are important, you will want to choose how to invest your time. Therefore, you can't afford to ignore time management.

The Resource of Time

Time is one of the five most important resources available to us. The others are information, people, money, and physical resources. If you skillfully control all resources except time, you still will not make the most of any of them. When you become highly skilled in controlling your time, you will be investing time for maximum return and will be able to make the most of all your other resources as well. **This makes time your most valuable resource.**

Three Reasons to Manage Time

There are three additional important reasons for managing time. Let's look at each of them.

1 Wasting Time Causes Stress

Many timewasters induce stress. There are **Seven Danger Signals** which indicate that an inability to manage time is causing stress.

- The belief that you are indispensable. No one else can do your work.

- No time for the important work you need and want to do. Daily crises consume your time, and the work that's your top priority must wait...and wait.

- Attempting too much at once by never saying, "No." You assume that you really can do it all.

- Unrelenting pressure. You always feel behind and have no hope of ever being on top of your job.

66 Your time is your life. What you do with your time determines what you do with your life. 99

- Habitual (not just occasional) long hours. Leaving the office at 5 o'clock has become a dream. Ten- to twelve-hour days are the norm, not the exception.

- Feeling guilty leaving work on time.

- Taking worry and problems home. Physically, you've left the office but you're preoccupied. The worries of the day take precedence over your home, family, and life.

If any of these seven signals are present in your life, stress from improper time management is affecting your work and minimizing your effectiveness. If you misuse your time, you pay the price and the cost is high. It even can set you up for illness. The well-documented correlation between stress and illness underscores the lifelong importance of managing yourself and your time.

Take a Moment...

List any of the **Seven Danger Signals** that play a role in your life.

_____

_____

_____

Which danger signal has the greatest impact on your life? What is the most effective step you can take to reduce its impact?

_____

_____

2 Managing Time Improves Productivity

Long hours do not ensure productivity. Past a certain point, the effectiveness of any effort declines rapidly as more and more hours are put in.

Eliminating your top three timewasters (which you'll define in Chapter Four) can free at least two hours per day. When **those two hours** are invested in **your top priority**, the dramatic increase in your productivity will leave you with one question, "Why on Earth did I wait so long?"

3 Managing Time Improves Your Quality of Life

Getting full value for your time means planning personal time and leisure into your schedule — quality time that you may never enjoy if you leave it to chance. It also means that you make the most of those personal hours by managing your work hours effectively so your mind is at ease.

An Example of Success

Bruce Peterson, as part of a time management seminar, targeted doubling his sales and his family time. It took him two years to achieve both goals. The first year he increased his income by 50 percent and took a four-week vacation with his family instead of two weeks. The second year he doubled his original income and increased his vacation time to six weeks. Bruce attributes this amazing record to setting demanding goals and to improving his time-control techniques.

" Time is on your side the moment you organize it. "

Take a Moment...

What reasons do *you* have for managing your time more effectively?

_____

_____

_____

What Is Time?

Aristotle said, "We all talk about time as though we understand it, but when we are asked to define it, we cannot." As part of the *Time Tactics® Process,* we define time as **a dimension within which things change.** At the end of every hour, your life has changed. What you did with that hour determines whether your life has changed for better or for worse. Learning the principles of the process enables you to choose what happens during that hour and to control the change.

The important question to ask yourself is, **"What is the best use of my time right now?"** The answer to this question lies in your choice of goals. Choosing goals means setting a standard for what you want to accomplish.

So, in the *Time Tactics® Process,* time is defined not only as **a dimension within which things change**, but also as **the medium through which goals are accomplished**. Every thought and every action required to achieve goals takes place in time. Every thought and action uses time. None of your goals — personal or professional — can ever be achieved after you have run out of time. When your time is up, you're done.

> Time is a dimension within which things change.
>
> Time also is the medium through which goals are accomplished.
>
> Time is your most *precious* resource.

Characteristics of Time

Of the five most important resources available to us (time, information, people, money, and physical resources), time has characteristics not shared with any of the others. They are:

- **Universal**

  Time is distributed equally. Everyone has the same limited amount.

- **Invariable**

  Time moves at a fixed rate. Time neither flies nor drags, although it may seem as if it does.

- **Unstorable**

  Time cannot be saved. It must be spent. If its use is unplanned, time will be wasted.

- **Irretrievable**

  You cannot postpone the expenditure of time. And once it's gone, you can't get it back.

- **Indivisible**

  Time and life are inseparable. Every thought, feeling, and action uses time.

66 Every thought, feeling, and action uses time. 99

13

Paradoxes of Time

Our personal experiences with time often force us to draw sets of conclusions which seem to contradict each other. They set up a paradox in which it is difficult to see how both conclusions can be true. Yet, on closer examination, the conclusions often are both correct. For example, "No one has enough time; yet everyone has all there is."

Often, one of the statements in a paradox is based on conventional wisdom, while the other statement challenges that wisdom by pointing out a deeper truth. "No one has enough time," is the conventional observation, while "Everyone has all there is," points out a deeper truth. Understanding these paradoxes is an important first step in the challenge of learning to manage our time and ourselves.

> 66 **No one has enough time; yet everyone has all there is.** 99

Take a Moment...

Consider the following paradoxes of time and explain the effect each one has on *your* life.

Time cannot be managed. We can only manage ourselves.

Is time the problem, or are we?

Those who don't take the time to do something right must make the time to do it over.

Should we do it right the first time?

Take a Moment... *(continued)*

Doing a job right is efficient.
Doing the right job right is effective.

If a task is the wrong one, it doesn't matter whether it is done right or wrong. If it's the right task, it matters a great deal.

The more hours people work,
the more time they assume they have to finish.

The more hours people work, the more fatigued they become — so they slow down. Long hours feed on themselves, making everything take longer.

The Bad News and the Good News

The bad news is that no one has enough time to do *everything* he or she would like. This does not mean time and self-management are hopeless. It does mean we must choose. We must learn to make the most of this precious resource. Managing time is never a luxury used only by people who have "time to plan." It is an imperative for everyone who wants time to succeed and time to live well.

The good news is that everyone has all the time there is — people trained in time and self-management, and people who have never heard of time and self-management. So, those who learn how to manage themselves in relation to time are more *effective.* Not simply the *busiest*, not simply the most *efficient* in completing any and all tasks, but the most *effective* in achieving the goals they have chosen.

> **" Some people seem to have more time than others; yet everyone has the same amount. "**

Take a Moment...

Ask yourself how much *more* time would you need to do everything *you* want to do in life.

25 percent more?   50 percent more?   75 percent more?

The problem is that while you may be certain you need more time, you are not going to get it. That leaves you with one alternative: **Learn to invest the time you have for maximum return.** The key to doing this reflects back to the concepts of commitment, choice, and control — the *Time Tactics® Process.*

The *Time Tactics® Process*

Time management is about making a commitment that will allow you to make choices. This concept is so basic, yet so important. But it is ignored daily by intelligent people who set their Number One Priority aside at the drop of a hat. When they do so, they **lose control** of their day. These days can add up to a lifetime. When people finally understand that they have a choice, they choose to work on their Number One Priority every day. And that makes all the difference.

> **The Number One Principle of Time Management**
>
> Identify your Number One Priority and get it done first. This is true for each hour and each day, as well as for your long-range plan. Remember to ask, "What is the best use of my time right now?"

"Get number one done first" is the most powerful phrase in time management.

- *Number one* means you've set priorities.
- *Get Done* means you're emphasizing results — not activity.
- *First* means you're setting deadlines.

The key to successful time management is to do the most important task first, giving it your full concentration to the exclusion of everything else.

A highly successful securities executive in London insists that the most important career lesson he has learned is to keep his desk clear of everything except his top priority for the day.

It's a simple idea that's very hard to do. We're all human and have a strong urge for instant gratification. We crave the feeling of success, of having accomplished something definite. So we tend to start our day with a task that's easy and quick. That's a surefire recipe for frittering away two, perhaps three, high-energy hours. One quick-and-easy task leads to another. We've all lived through it.

Consider, however, if you're always working on your Number One Priority, you'll always be doing what you have decided is most important. If you don't get everything done, you still will have accomplished your most important priority. And, you will be in a position to say, "No," to interruptions because you are working on your highest priority.

The *Time Tactics® Process* shows you how to do that. It provides a complete process for managing **your most precious resource — time.** It gives you the tools to implement that process successfully.

You will learn to apply the three concepts of the *Time Tactics® Process:* **commitment, choice,** and **control**. You will also learn to use the basic principles of the process. They are:

- **Set goals.**

- **Understand the major timewasters and their solutions.**

- **Make the commitment to fill in the Time Log.**

- **Identify your top personal timewasters.**

- **Develop your Personal Action Plan.**
  - √ **Eliminate your top timewasters.**
  - √ **Plot your personal energy cycle.**
  - √ **Develop your Ideal Day.**

- **Plan each day before you start it.**

- **Identify your Number One Priority and get it done first.**

Remember, you have as much time as the most successful person you know. You, too, can achieve your highest potential, if you apply the principles in this book. Once you have defined real success for yourself, take your most valuable resource — **time** — and invest it where it will do the most good.

When you make the commitment to choose what you do with your time, you take control of your life. If you don't, others will do it for you. It's your choice.

Chapter One Review

Please complete the following questions. Answers appear on page 92.

1. Time is a dimension within which things _____. Time is also the medium through which _____ are accomplished. Finally, time is your most precious _____.

2. When you make the _____ to choose what you do with your time, you take _____ of your life.

3. What are the three reasons to manage time?

   _____

   _____

   _____

Indicate whether you think each of the following statements is **True** or **False.**

4. _____ People trained in time management have more time than people without time management training.

5. _____ Time management is a luxury, mainly used by people who have time to plan.

6. _____ Time cannot be managed separately from those who are using it.

The Role of Goals in Time Management

Chapter Objectives:

After you have read this chapter and have completed the interactive exercises, you should be able to:

- ☑ Describe the Choose-and-Control System.
- ☑ State the relationships between goals and time.
- ☑ Describe the characteristics of goals.
- ☑ Define success for you and your organization.
- ☑ Define your on-the-job success by relating it to the success of your organization.
- ☑ Translate your definitions of personal, professional, and organizational success into concrete, measurable goals, with deadlines.

Goals Provide Direction

Until we have established our goals, much of our activity is pointless. Without goals, we have no reason to organize ourselves and our time because we're not going anywhere in particular. It then makes no difference how long anything takes. Every activity is of equal value.

But once we have identified our goals, we are able to judge the effectiveness of our time choices. Did our choices make real progress toward our goals—or were they distractions?

Goals and time are your keys to success. You achieve success — as defined in your goals — through the medium of time.

> **Choice — the establishment of goals — is at the heart of the Choose-and-Control system to managing your time and your life. The first step in managing your time is to decide what you want.**

Choose-and-Control System

You've made the commitment, now you're ready for the Choose-and-Control System. The first step in taking charge of your life is to **choose** long-range goals. You make hundreds of choices each day. Most you hardly notice, starting with the decision to push or not to push the snooze button for an extra ten minutes of sleep. By the time you go to bed sixteen hours later, you also have made pivotal choices — good or bad — which affect your real priorities. But unless your first choices are to identify long-term goals and to set priorities, the hundreds of other daily choices you make are simply random acts.

Once you select goals, you can decide how to invest your time so that you get the most out of your day, week, month, year — and your life. By keeping these goals in mind, you have a standard for setting your daily priorities.

Control is the means by which you achieve those priorities. It means that you plan, you work, you measure progress, and you take corrective action to ensure that your goals are met.

Once you choose goals and control how you invest your time, you are well under way to managing yourself and your time successfully.

> **❝ We can know whether what we are doing is absurd only after we have identified the goals we seek to achieve. ❞**
>
> *Charles Hughes,*
> *Past President*
> *Texas Instruments*

What Is the Relationship Between Goals and Time?

Every goal requires some amount of time, however small, to be achieved. Because the amount of time in your life is limited, you cannot achieve an infinite number of goals. Some of the many goals you would like to achieve will not be accomplished. The question is, "Who decides which goals you'll actually achieve?" In the Choose-and-Control System, you decide which goals you will achieve and you control what happens to your time.

> **If you don't manage your time, you'll never achieve your goals. But if you don't have goals, you don't need time because you aren't going anywhere. Top goal achievers are always top time managers.**
>
> ***...Lloyd Loffet***

CASE STUDY

Consider Robert Owen. He is a person of enormous charm and great wealth, heading several successful businesses in Australia. When asked the secret of his success, he replied simply, "Goals." He examined these areas when setting his personal and professional goals and asked some hard-hitting questions.

Private Versus Business Life: What ratio of time should be spent on each?

Health: What standard do I want to maintain?

Personal Relationships: How can they be improved?

Education: What new fields should be pursued?

Wealth: How much should be sought?

Change of Job and/or Career: When and under what circumstances is a change desirable?

Social and Religious Life: What steps should be taken to improve quality?

Even if you don't agree with all of his priorities, you can see that Robert Owen is a man who has looked at his life and decided what is important to him.

Characteristics of Effective Goals

Effective goals share the following seven characteristics:

1. Owned by Those Affected

Goals which are defined by those who are affected are much more likely to be carried out with enthusiasm and commitment. People have a better understanding of a goal when they have participated in its development. They also are far more motivated to carry it out.

When people and organizations together develop goals consistent with their *mutual* success, they have taken the first step toward highly effective time management. They have created a standard for evaluating whether or not their activities make sense and whether or not their use of time makes sense.

2. Demanding

Goals which are not demanding are barely goals at all. Nothing is more motivating than setting demanding goals which reflect your values and then figuring out how to achieve them systematically.

3. **Achievable**

Goals must be feasible enough for you to achieve them. If you set goals which are so unrealistic you have no hope of attaining them, you have set yourself up for frustration and failure. However, if you have an "impossible dream" that you really want, don't abandon it. Break it up into smaller, more realistic, attainable sub-goals and begin achieving them, one at a time.

4. **Measurable**

Your goals must be measurable so you can judge your progress and so you know when you have succeeded. **Measuring progress is also an excellent motivator and enables you to correct your course when necessary.**

5. **Deadlines**

Goals need deadlines. Otherwise they will be shifted aside for whatever seems pressing at the moment.

6. **Written**

Goals should be written so they won't be forgotten. One person said, "Out of sight, out of mind." Another reminded us that, "The palest ink is better than the best memory."

7. **Flexible**

Goals must be flexible enough to accommodate changing conditions.

Three Kinds of Goals

Most people would like to achieve success in at least three important areas:

- In their **personal lives**
- Within the **organizations** for which they work
- In their **long-range career** aspirations

But unless they set effective goals in each of these areas, they are unlikely to succeed and enjoy their full potential. They will lack the commitment, the time, the direction, and the long-term motivation to actually achieve what they want.

You will find the payoff well worth the effort if you invest time in learning to write effective goals in each of these categories. It will enable you to think about and examine your goals in all areas of your life — so they are in sync with each other and not at cross-purposes.

First, define success in each area — the condition you want to achieve. Then develop goals to get there — goals which target your definitions of success.

1 Personal Goals

Goals express your values. Personal goals which work well for you are based on your own definition of success.

The best general definition of success is progressive achievement of your goals through doing *your best*. If you are able to "get by" and still "succeed," you will never experience the deep satisfaction which comes from doing *your best* to achieve your own demanding goals.

Take a Moment...

Use the space below to define **personal** success for you.
To be successful in my personal life, I want to:

1. _____

2. _____

3. _____

2 Career/Organizational Goals

Career goals which work well for you and your organization are based on your own definition of professional success, as well as your organization's definition of success. When you develop goals which target both these definitions of success, the two results are:

- *Sustainability of the relationship between you and your organization.*
- *Maximum achievement for both you and your organization over the long run.*

Take a Moment...

Use the space below to define **professional** success for you.
To be successful in my professional life, I want to:

1. _____

2. _____

3. _____

Take a Moment...

Use the space below to define success for your organization.

1. _____

2. _____

3. _____

Now define your professional success by relating it to the success of your organization. First, look at these three examples:

*Increasing **my sales by 25 percent** in the next three months will bring **my organization 10 percent closer to its sales target** for the quarter and qualify me for a bonus.*

*Improving my time management skills to the point where I can achieve in six hours the same results which now require seven will give me one hour per day or **five hours per week to invest in mastering the new quality processes** my company is adopting. Success in mastering the time management skills and the new quality processes also will give me **additional long-range career skills.***

*Taking a seminar on listening skills will help me **work more effectively with my coworkers** and also help me **understand my family better.***

Take a Moment...

Now, it's your turn. Develop a current example which relates your professional success to the success of your organization:

_____

_____

2

Take a Moment...

Using your definition of personal success from page 26, develop your three most important personal long-range goals for the next five years. Remember the characteristics of effective goals described on pages 23-24.

1. _____

_____

2. _____

_____

3. _____

_____

Now, using your definition of professional success from page 26, develop your three most important professional long-range goals for the next five years which meet the characteristics of effective goals (page 23-24) and which target both your professional success and the success of your organization.

1. _____

_____

2. _____

_____

3. _____

_____

3 Long-Range/Interim Goals

You now have set personal and professional long-range goals. Because five years seems to be as far as most people can realistically plan ahead, you may find the following categories useful as you continue the goal development process:

√ **Long-range goals** — What you want to achieve in the next **five years.**

√ **Intermediate goals** — What you want to achieve in the next **two years.**

√ **Short-term goals** — What you want to achieve in the **next year.**

√ **Monthly goals** — What you want to achieve each **month.**

√ **Weekly goals** — What you want to achieve each **week.**

√ **Daily tasks** — What you want to achieve **each day.**

√ **Priorities** — Daily tasks ranked in order of importance.

Review the long-range goals you developed. Then, working backward from those goals, develop the interim goals — both personal and professional — with deadlines, you will need to achieve by the end of two years, this year, by the end of this month, by the end of this week, and by the end of tomorrow.

This is the way Marcia developed one of her long-range goals:

Long-range goal — Become vice president of the division within five years.

Two-year goal — Become general manager of the division.

One-year goal — Become assistant general manager.

Six-month goal — Complete all training requirements for assistant general manager.

This week — See training director and register for all relevant courses.

Today — Review written goals already established by the division to ensure that my goals are consistent with them.

Please make three photocopies of this page and complete one for each of your personal long-range goals defined on page 26.

Take a Moment...

Translate Your <u>Personal</u> Long-Range Goals into Interim Goals

Long-range goal

_____

Two-year goal

_____

One-year goal

_____

Six-month goal

_____

This week

_____

Today

_____

Remember, you want to do things with your life, rather than merely drift along. So hang in here. **Connecting your long-range goals to your daily priorities is part of the *Time Tactics® Process.*** Give it your full effort and you won't regret it.

Please make three photocopies of this page and complete one for each of your professional long-range goals defined on page 26.

Take a Moment...

Translate Your <u>Professional</u> Long-Range Goals into Interim Goals

Long-range goal

_____

Two-year goal

_____

One-year goal

_____

Six-month goal

_____

This week

_____

Today

_____

> # Goals and time are your keys to success.

Your Time Management Blueprint

With your most important goals in hand, you now can carry out the remaining processes in this book. As you come to understand the causes of and solutions to specific timewasters, as you develop a Personal Action Plan, and as you develop your Daily Plan, you will not be merely executing exercises. You will be **constructing a real blueprint for managing your goals, your time, and your life.**

Chapter Two Review

Please complete the following questions. Answers appear on page 92.

Indicate whether you think statements 1 through 5 are **True** or **False.**

1. _____ In the Choose-and-Control System, choice is the selection of goals.

2. _____ Goals are based on our values and our definitions of success.

3. _____ Once goals are identified, we are able to judge the effectiveness of our time choices.

4. _____ Flexible goals and deadlined goals are incompatible.

5. _____ Measuring progress toward goals is a common pitfall which leads to unnecessary frustration.

6. List the seven characteristics of effective goals.

_____

_____

_____

_____

_____

_____

_____

7. Name two results which are achieved when you target goals for your success and the success of your organization.

_____

_____

CHAPTER THREE

Discovering Where Time Goes—A Tool You Cannot Do Without

Chapter Objectives:

After you have read this chapter and have completed the interactive exercises, you should be able to:

- ☑ Understand why the Time Log is the tool you cannot do without.
- ☑ Know how to execute your Time Log.
- ☑ Know how to analyze your Time Log.

Good time management means getting full value for your investment of time.

Now that you've established your goals, you know where you are going. The next step is to discover where your *time* goes. This step is crucial.

Where <u>Does</u> Time Go?

Like the rest of us, you, undoubtedly, think you know where your time goes, but chances are, you don't. One day it flies. Another day it crawls. And when that boring meeting finally ends, you're delighted to hear from unexpected callers. By afternoon you're frustrated with looming deadlines. And by evening, your Number One Priority for today has become your Number One Priority for tomorrow.

You're doomed to repeat this scenario over and over unless you find out **where your time went.** This chapter will help you do just that. It provides the single most powerful tool available for achieving control of your time and your life — the Time Log.

A Time Log is a detailed, minute-by-minute record of your time.
- It allows you to see with breathtaking clarity just how much time you waste.
- It gives you facts, not half-remembered history or excuses.
- It hits you with hard data you can use to turn your time and your life around.
- If you complete the Time Log exactly as instructed, you will be surprised by the results.

The painful task of changing your habits requires far more conviction than you can get from learning about the time management experience of other people. The real conviction that you need to change your habits comes only when you are confronted with the stark truths revealed in your own personal Time Log.

The Time Log Is Research You Need

To begin having the Time Log work for you, carefully follow these instructions. Make at least three copies of the Time Log on page 38, and complete your Time Log for each day. See the sample Time Log printed on pages 39-40 for assistance.

1. Make the commitment to keep the Time Log for three consecutive full work days. Five consecutive work days would be ideal to measure a work week. This commitment will provide you with the valuable information you need to invest your time for maximum return.

3

2. At the top of each page, write the date and the key goals for that day, along with deadlines for their completion.

3. In the space provided on the Time Log, note the priority for each entry.
    1   Both very important *and* very urgent
    2   Either important *or* urgent
    3   Routine detail
    4   Trivial

    At the end of the day, you will see what percentage of your time was spent on top-priority work.

4. Be very specific. If you simply write "phone calls," you won't be able to tell at the end of the day which were necessary and which were timewasters. You also won't be able to judge whether the time spent on them was warranted.

5. Record each activity throughout the day *as soon as it happens,* not at fixed intervals, such as thirty minutes. You simply miss too much that way. Record all interruptions, no matter how small. Do this all day; don't try to catch up at the end of the day. You won't remember, even if you think you will. What's more, there may be the temptation to gloss over items.

6. Whenever your attention shifts from one activity to another, write down the cause of the shift, however trivial. Don't skip over daydreaming, socializing, or brief interruptions just because they seem minor at the time. One thing you are trying to determine is how much of your *total* time is frittered away in such minor activities.

7. In the "Comments" column, note what you could have done more effectively, or perhaps not at all.

8. Use shortcut signs and abbreviations, for example, phone call out: c>, phone call in: c<.

9. Plan time to analyze your time logs at the end of the research period.

10. Be totally honest in your research or it won't help you.

11. Be prepared for some surprises!

12. Write the date three days from now — or five days from now — when you will use your Time Log to complete a crucial part of the *Time Tactics® Process:* Analyzing Your Time Log and Using the Results (page 41). Date:_____

Also, post this date above your work area. Remember, commitment is an essential element of this process. The return on your investment of time, with committed follow-through, will astonish you and change your life.

After you've had an opportunity to complete your Time Log, continue with the rest of this chapter.

66 **Time losses add up quickly, like interest on consumer debt.** 99

DAILY TIME LOG

Name: _____   Date: _____

Daily Goals: **Deadline:**

(1) _____ _____   (4) _____ _____
(2) _____ _____   (5) _____ _____
(3) _____ _____   (6) _____ _____

Priority: 1 - Important & Urgent; 2 - Important or Urgent; 3 - Routine Detail; 4 - Trivial

TIME	ACTIVITY	TIME USED	PRIORITY	COMMENT/DISPOSITION

Sample Time Log

DAILY TIME LOG

Name: _E. Donnelly_   Date: _Sept. 16_

Daily Goals: **Deadline:**

(1) _complete mgmt. review_   _5:00 pm_   (4) _prepare for staff meeting_   _9:30 am_
(2) _prepare sales summary_   _1:00 pm_   (5) _____   _____
(3) _dev. service report_   _1:00 pm_   (6) _____   _____

Priority: 1 - Important and Urgent; 2 - Important or Urgent; 3 - Routine Detail; 4 - Trivial

TIME	ACTIVITY	TIME USED	PRIORITY	COMMENT/DISPOSITION
8:00	get coffee; read w.s. journal	20	4	can read at lunch; first 20 min. wasted
8:30	review plan for today	15	1	well spent; found 2 problems to talk to Helen about
8:45	misc. notes to Helen	5	1	good use of time
8:50	B C called	15	4	unnec. interruption
9:05	B B called	15	4	ditto
9:20	dictation, Helen	45	2	not really organized for this dictation
10:05	read and separate mail	30	4	Helen can do; have her sort and prioritize
10:32	boss came by; chat re: trip (personal)	16	4	act busy; be candid when boss drops in
10:51	coffee	9	4	not necessary - habit
11:00	staff meeting	60	2??	could have been done in 30 min
12:00	sign mail	20	4	Helen could sign routine mail
12:20	lunch	65	4	could have met w/ boss at lunch to discuss sales report
1:25	complete sales summary for 2:00 meeting	30	1	urgent now - left to last minute

DAILY TIME LOG

Name: _____ *E. Donnelly* _____   Date: ____ *Sept. 16* ____

Daily Goals: **Deadline:**

(1) *complete mgmt. review*   *5:00 pm*   (4) *prepare for staff meeting*   *9:30 am*

(2) *prepare sales summary*   *1:00 pm*   (5) _____ _____

(3) *dev. service report*   *1:00 pm*   (6) _____ _____

Priority: 1 - Important and Urgent; 2 - Important or Urgent; 3 - Routine Detail; 4 - Trivial

TIME	ACTIVITY	TIME USED	PRIORITY	COMMENT/DISPOSITION
1:55	called JD re: personnel	5	4	ditto, this could wait
2:00	mtg. w/boss—sales sum.	45	2	if written report had been submitted earlier, boss could have reviewed—then this mtg. could be cut to 15 minutes or even
2:30	boss oks delay on service report			eliminated if he had returned it to me w/questions —30 min. wasted.
3:07	RM dropped in, questions on info for new system	8	4	refer to Hank
3:15	go for coffee	15	4	don't need it!
3:30	distrib. meeting	60	4	attended out of habit; some questions to me that Hank could handle; from now on leave these meetings
4:30	worked on mgt. review	3	1	this was #1 for day but left until end/permitted interruptions
4:33	interruption by TM re: staff mtg.	7	4	could easily wait until next mtg.
4:40	back to mgt. review	15	1	not much accomplished
4:55	call pers. re: Brown — too late	5	2	procrastination killed this one.
5:10	home			where did day go???

Analyzing Your Time Log and Using the Results

Congratulations on completing your Time Log! Your efforts will be well rewarded.

Now that you've recorded in detail your use of time for a minimum of three consecutive working days, you are ready to analyze your Time Log, identify your top timewasters, and develop solutions.

With all your log sheets for each day spread out in order, answer the following questions.

1. Each day, what time did you start on your Number One Priority? Could you have started sooner?

    _____

2. Each day, did anything distract you from your Number One Priority? Could you have avoided the distraction? Once distracted, did you recover immediately and return to the task at once? Explain.

    _____

3. Each day, did you completely achieve your Number One Priority? If not, what percentage of your Number One Priority did you complete?

    _____

4. Each day, did you completely achieve your Number Two Priority? If not, what percentage of your Number Two Priority did you complete?

    _____

5. Each day, did you completely achieve your Number Three Priority? If not, what percentage of your Number Three Priority did you complete?

_____

6. Each day, how many hours did you spend on:

	Priority One	Priority Two	Priority Three	Priority Four
Day 1				
Day 2				
Day 3				

What percentage of the total hours logged for all days did you spend on each priority? _____

7. What was your longest period of totally uninterrupted time? (Don't count lunches or meetings.)

_____

8. What things did you do that you should not have been doing? Could they have been delegated?

_____

9. How could you have done what you were doing more effectively? more simply? in less detail?

_____

10. During the total logged time, how many interruptions were for items more important than the interrupted task? _____

11. During the total logged time, how many interruptions were for items less important than the interrupted task?_____

12. During the total logged time, count the interruptions by each of the following and total the time in each category:

Phone _____

Visitors _____

Yourself (include daydreaming) _____

Coworkers _____

Boss _____

Assistant _____

Unplanned meetings_____

Client_____

Crises _____

Looking for items _____

Paperwork _____

13. How much time was spent in meetings? Was it productive? Which priorities did it further?

_____

14. Which of your communications with others were important enough to be worth it?

_____

15. Which communications took too long?

_____

16. How much time was spent waiting? What did you do while you waited?

_____

17. Which kind of interruption occurred the greatest number of times?

_____

18. Which kind of interruption wasted the greatest total amount of time?

_____

19. Which kind of interruption do you think had the greatest impact on your top priorities?

   _____

20. What specific changes does your Time Log suggest you should make in order to accomplish your top priorities?

   _____

Future Uses of Your Time Log

Periodic Log. After you have analyzed your Time Log and implemented the rest of the Choose-and-Control system, you will want to fill in a Periodic Log four times a year to:

- Maintain awareness of your new time habits.

- Prevent regression into your old time habits.

Occasional Specific Targeted Log. Use this log to:

- Determine the seriousness of particular timewasters.

- Measure your progress in developing your new time habits.

Continual Specific Targeted Log. Many successful time managers use this to:

- Provide a continuous self-disciplining tool.

- Monitor ongoing effectiveness in utilizing time.

- Trigger immediate self-correction.

An Example of Success

A senior AT&T executive in New Jersey used the Continual Time Log every working day. He had discovered that it took very little time and alerted him immediately when time was being wasted. A self-correcting tendency always set in immediately to remedy the situation.

This executive called the Continual·Time Log "the most powerful self-disciplining tool" he had ever encountered.

Now that you have analyzed your Time Log, turn to Chapter Four, which will help you understand your timewasters and identify solutions for them.

Putting Yourself in Control—

Understanding and Handling Timewasters

Chapter Objectives:

After you have read this chapter and have completed the interactive exercises, you should be able to:

- ☑ Understand the three major categories of timewasters:
  - **—Lack of Planning.**
  - **—Lack of Self-Management.**
  - **—Lack of Control over the Work Environment.**
- ☑ Understand the specific timewasters in each of these three major categories.
- ☑ Identify solutions to these specific timewasters.

What Is a Timewaster?

A timewaster is anything that decreases your productivity and your effectiveness. Usually, a timewaster causes a shift in attention away from your Number One Priority. Many timewasters are a form of interruption. As Dr. Kenneth Dunn puts it, "Nothing exceeds the power of interruption to kill time."

There are three major categories of timewasters: lack of planning, lack of self-management, and lack of control over the work environment. Let's review each one.

1 Lack of Planning

The first major category of timewasters is **Lack of Planning.** Those who think they are too busy to plan will always waste more time managing by crisis. Even on calm days, their energies will be scattered. And if they achieve their Number One Priority, it will be by accident.

Sometimes people claim they have been successful without planning. Once they invest time in careful planning, however, they are astounded to see the investment pay off many times over in increased effectiveness. One hour spent in effective planning usually saves three in execution — and achieves better results. Add up those hours. Using a 40-hour week, the total additional work time made available to you through effective planning is four months per year.

People who don't take time to plan *waste* time; people who make time to plan *invest* time.

Within the category of Lack of Planning, there are several specific concerns that have been proven to waste time over and over.

Lack of Goals/Unclear Objectives

This timewaster is listed first because the planning process begins with the careful establishment of long-range and short-range goals. You carried out this process on pages 30-31 when you developed personal and professional goals consistent with your success and the success of your organization.

Once you have made the hard choices in establishing real long-range and short-range personal and professional goals, you have standards for focusing your time. You have standards for yearly, monthly, weekly, and daily planning. You have a basis for determining your Number One Priority each day. And you have a powerful motivator to replace old timewasters with new habits which can turn your life and your time around.

66 Remember, chance favors the prepared mind. 99

4

Lack of Daily Priorities

Some of us lack the self-discipline necessary to make a written plan with priorities each day. Without priorities, it's easy to waste time. The significance of the Daily Plan in the *Time Tactics® Process* is that it forces you to set priorities. This is planning at its core. Here's how it works: At the end of each day, you invest fifteen minutes to develop the next day's written plan *with priorities*. The next morning, do the Number One Priority first — and that means *first* — not after checking the mail, not after clearing away small jobs. Make a commitment to follow this procedure for one month. You will find it enormously beneficial. Enlist the support of those around you, in your office and at home.

How do priorities differ from goals? A goal is a predetermined result — something you intend to achieve over the long term. A priority is a ranking (Number One, Number Two, Number Three, and so on) of your daily tasks. **So the tasks related to your most important goals become your top priorities.**

As you prioritize your daily tasks, evaluate them according to their **long-range importance** and their **short-range urgency.** A simple Priority Matrix, similar to the example on the next page, is helpful.

> 66 **Nothing approaches the motivating power of setting demanding goals and then systematically measuring progress toward achieving them.** 99

SAMPLE PRIORITY MATRIX

TASK	LONG-RANGE IMPORTANCE	SHORT-RANGE URGENCY	TOTAL	PRIORITY
marketing plan	1	1	2	1
department bdgt.	2	1	3	2
conf. agenda	3	2	5	4
sales report	2	3	5	4
board minutes	1	2	3	2

Using the above as an example, complete the Priority Matrix on page 50, using your own priorities. On the matrix, list ten tasks you should do tomorrow. Using *1* as most important or urgent, *2* as medium importance or urgency, and *3* as lower importance or urgency, rate each task and total the ratings.

With this information, rank your tasks under the heading "Priority." Total the three categories. You now have the information which will enable you to implement the most important principle of time management. The category with the *lowest* total is your Number One Priority, and it should be done *first*.

After using the matrix for a few weeks, you'll be able to do the process in your head. Soon it will become second nature. Once in a while, go back to the matrix to prevent backsliding.

4

PRIORITY MATRIX

TASK	LONG-RANGE IMPORTANCE	SHORT-RANGE URGENCY	TOTAL	PRIORITY

The Tyranny of the Urgent

An urgent task is one that must be done now. But the fact that a task is urgent says nothing about how important it is. It may be vital to your long-range goals or have little or no relevance. Sometimes you must attend to the urgent. But don't mistake the urgent for the important or you will risk not achieving your long-range goals.

If you master the preceding practical approach to prioritizing so that it becomes second nature, **you can look back at the end of the year with the real satisfaction that you have not sacrificed long-range importance for short-term urgency.**

Practice Developing Daily Priorities

Examine the Sample Daily Plan on the next page. Then on page 53, in the spaces provided at the top, write your daily goals. (You may photocopy this page, if you want to save the blank Sample Daily Plan.) At the bottom, list everything you have to do each day. Evaluate each task against the standard of your goals, prioritize it, and give it a deadline.

Next, block out periods of time to achieve your daily priorities, placing the most important first.

Big jobs won't be completed in one day. But if you decide to work on project number one from 8 AM to 10 AM, you may decide to complete the first phase of it by the 10 o'clock deadline.

The real reward comes when you see how much you have accomplished by the end of the day.

4

> **Concentrating your efforts on the critical 20 percent of your tasks will produce around 80 percent of your results. That's why it's so important to prioritize.**

SAMPLE DAILY PLAN

FEBRUARY   *WEEK 8*   19__

Monday 17	Tuesday 18	Wednesday 19	Thursday 20	Friday 21	Saturday 22
Tasks	*Tasks*	*Tasks*	*Tasks*	*Tasks*	
1. Draft Video Costs	1. Slides	1. Review pkg. in house	1. Final Draft Video	1. Graphics	8:00 Sam—tennis
2. Staff Meeting	2. Back Correspond.	2. Sam's Proposal			
3. Newton Proposal		3. Final Draft			

Appointments	*Appointments*	*Appointments*	*Appointments*	*Appointments*	
8:00 am	8:00 am	8:00 am	8:00 am	8:00 am	
9:00 am	9:00 am	9:00 am	9:00 am no appts.	9:00 am no appts.	
Tom - Recruiting	Meet with Sue				
10:00 am	10:00 am	10:00 am	10:00 am	10:00 am	
	Staff Meeting				
11:00 am	11:00 am	11:00 am	11:00 am	11:00 am	1:00 Shopping - Lea
12:00 pm	12:00 pm	12:00 pm	12:00 pm	12:00 pm	
Nevins Eatery			Sam at Fox's		
1:00 pm	1:00 pm	1:00 pm	1:00 pm	1:00 pm	
	Review Videos				
2:00 pm	2:00 pm	2:00 pm	2:00 pm	2:00 pm	
		Mary - Printing		ck/Harry - Videos	
3:00 pm	3:00 pm	3:00 pm	3:00 pm	3:00 pm	
	Tom - Presentation		Review with Tom		
4:00 pm	4:00 pm	4:00 pm	4:00 pm	4:00 pm	
Agenda to Typing	Final Draft				
5:00 pm	5:00 pm	5:00 pm	5:00 pm	5:00 pm	Sunday 23
					Set VCR Ch. 13
6:00 pm	6:00 pm	6:00 pm	6:00 pm	6:00 pm	@ 10 pm
		Cocktails - Sims			
7:00 pm	7:00 pm	7:00 pm	7:00 pm	7:00 pm	

To Do:	*To Do:*	*To Do:*	*To Do:*	*To Do:*	
Jim - Editing	Call JB	Order Jerry's Cake	For lunch w/Sam,	Stop at store for Lea	
		Sims 555-1212	Figures on Proposal		
Read Jacobsen Article	Sam	12 Park - Eatery 8pm	Needs List		

DAILY PLAN

*MONTH*_____   *WEEK*_____   *19*__

Day/Date Goals	Day/Date Goals	Day/Date Goals	Day/Date Goals	Day/Date Goals	Day/Date Goals
_____	_____	_____	_____	_____	_____
_____	_____	_____	_____	_____	_____
_____	_____	_____	_____	_____	_____
_____	_____	_____	_____	_____	_____

Appointments 8:00 am	Appointments 8:00 am	Appointments 8:00 am	Appointments 8:00 am	Appointments 8:00 am	Appointments 8:00 am
9:00 am	9:00 am	9:00 am	9:00 am	9:00 am	9:00 am
10:00 am	10:00 am	10:00 am	10:00 am	10:00 am	10:00 am
11:00 am	11:00 am	11:00 am	11:00 am	11:00 am	11:00 am
12:00 pm	12:00 pm	12:00 pm	12:00 pm	12:00 pm	12:00 pm
1:00 pm	1:00 pm	1:00 pm	1:00 pm	1:00 pm	1:00 pm
2:00 pm	2:00 pm	2:00 pm	2:00 pm	2:00 pm	2:00 pm
3:00 pm	3:00 pm	3:00 pm	3:00 pm	3:00 pm	3:00 pm
4:00 pm	4:00 pm	4:00 pm	4:00 pm	4:00 pm	4:00 pm
5:00 pm	5:00 pm	5:00 pm	5:00 pm	5:00 pm	5:00 pm
6:00 pm	6:00 pm	6:00 pm	6:00 pm	6:00 pm	6:00 pm
7:00 pm	7:00 pm	7:00 pm	7:00 pm	7:00 pm	7:00 pm

To Do:	To Do:	To Do:	To Do:	To Do:	To Do:

> 66 **Every interruption uses up not only its actual time, but also the recovery time needed to refocus on your task.**99

Shifting Priorities

Don't let interruptions shift your priorities. You are not required to respond to every interruption. Once you have identified the real priorities in your job and in your life, you have a standard for judging interruptions. If they will take you away from more important priorities, you need to remain in control. Don't let the interruption take control. Every interruption uses up not only its actual time, but also the *recovery time* needed to refocus on your task.

Learn the techniques later in this chapter for dealing with the timewasters, "Telephone Interruptions," "Drop-In Visitors," "Socializing," and the "Inability to Say, "No"." Also, pay particular attention to the ideas under "Lack of Self-Discipline."

Anytime in the future when your priorities are not being achieved, go back and fill in a Time Log to find out what's really going on.

Crisis Management

Without planning, you wait to see what crises hit you each day. After each crisis, if you fail to carry out evaluation, planning, and corrective action, you are doomed to repeat the process. Planning helps prevent crises.

Take the following quiz to find out how good you are at crisis prevention. If your score is below 18, try using some of the points listed in the quiz and then retake it three months from now.

Almost Never	= 0	Usually	= 3
Sometimes	= 1	Almost Always	= 4
Half the Time	= 2		

1. I anticipate things that can go wrong and take action to prevent them or to limit their consequences._____

2. I require regular progress reports on all major tasks so I can identify problems in time to take corrective action._____

3. Whenever goals and objectives have been set, I examine all reasonable alternatives for achieving them so I can determine which are least likely to generate crises._____

4. When managing crisis situations, I avoid overcommitment of resources by determining who and what are really needed to handle the situation._____

5. After a crisis, I ask those involved what happened and what steps can be taken to avoid a repetition. Then I implement suitable steps immediately._____

6. I build cushions into my day to allow time to respond to unforeseen crises._____

TOTAL: _____

Attempting Too Much

This timewaster is a classic illustration of the failure to choose. Without goals and priorities, you are left with the hopeless task of doing everything. No one, from Mother Theresa to Arnold Schwarzenegger, can do everything. If you try to be indispensable on all tasks, you may not do any of them well. Choose to perform those things you do well and delegate the rest. Determine which tasks contribute nothing to your goals. Discuss with your manager what he or she really wants you to do to ensure that your priorities are clear. Also, recognize that long-term success is more important than short-term impressions created by attempting everything. Ask yourself what you are really trying to prove. Assess your answer in the light of your long-range personal, career, and organizational goals.

Unrealistic Time Estimates

By now we all know that everything takes longer than it should, that nothing is as simple as it first seems, and that unexpected complications arise. Stop expecting miracles. Instead of promising what is impossible to deliver, build realistic cushions (20 to 50 percent) into your time estimates. Start early, so you can correct for mistakes and give yourself a break along the way.

Remember: Unrealistic deadlines cause haste, tension, and mistakes which then must be corrected. As a result, jobs take longer than if the deadlines had been realistic in the first place.

2 Lack of Self-Management

Lack of Self-Management is another broad category of timewasters. It can be broken down into the following areas of concern.

Lack of Self-Discipline

Human nature makes this timewaster a lifelong challenge for almost everyone. Its solutions are similar to the solutions for many other timewasters. For example: Planning encourages disciplined action. Setting priorities focuses effort on the most productive tasks. Realistic deadlines impose discipline, as do daily and weekly written plans, project control charts, and progress reports. Rewards, when checkpoints are successfully reached, improve self-discipline — but only if you refuse to enjoy the reward early —- more self-discipline!

Personal Disorganization

It should not be surprising that this timewaster is closely related to lack of self-discipline. You will never master this timewaster unless you have the self-discipline to (1) first invest the original time to get organized and (2) then schedule organizing time into every day. Use this daily organizing time to file, to enter on a computer, to delegate, to throw out — in short, to achieve each day a clean desk and an updated information system. The real key here is not to get behind. To stay current, **you must schedule organizing time every day.**

A Cluttered Desk and an Inadequate Filing System

These two timewasters often complement each other. When combined with other timewasters, the results are disastrous. The rationalization we all make is that in our own case the cluttered desk is justified. We are extremely busy people, carrying out important projects. And, besides, we are able to find things when we need them. The sad truth is that the person buried beneath the mountain of random notes, phone messages, file folders, lists, and unfinished reports is not managing goals, time, or self. Investing the time to get and stay organized is not really a choice. It's a question of long-range survival.

The number-one cure for this timewaster is to adopt a lifetime habit of filing material immediately so that it can be retrieved instantly. Don't let it pile up in stacks. Here are several types of filing systems.

- One system uses file folders numbered 1 to 31 to hold documents until the day they are needed. Each morning, that day's file folder is checked as part of the planning routine. After it is used, the material is filed in the appropriate subject file or discarded.

- A second system uses six folders labeled Today, This Week, One to Three Months, Three to Twelve Months, and Pending (date not yet known). At the end of the week, "This Week" should be empty.

- Yet another system uses color-coded folders to file material by areas of job responsibility.

Whichever system you choose, you should develop a coding system which routes papers to files for destroying after one month, after one year, after a project is completed, or for placing in a permanent file.

4

The best solution for personal disorganization is a planner/organizer system which provides a place for:

- Daily goals, appointments, and lower-priority to-dos.
- Control sheets for tracking major projects or objectives.
- Contact log, where key decisions and action items needing follow-up are recorded.
- Individual dividers for contacts with key people.
- Long-range plans and monthly goals.
- Alphabetical directory with phone, fax, and E-mail numbers, along with addresses.

Paperwork

The keys to solving this timewaster can be explained in two short sentences. **Handle it once. Do it now.** Surveys show that 80 percent of paperwork can be disposed of on the first handling. The average person disposes of only 20 percent! Take action before you put the piece of paper down. Answer on the original when you don't need a copy. If a file copy is necessary, make your notes on the original and photocopy it. Keep only what you need. Mark file copies to indicate their filing life. Don't reinvent the wheel. Save time when composing letters by using previous letters as templates for future tasks. Whenever you can, delegate.

Procrastination

Fear of failure is one big reason for this timewaster. If the task is complex or difficult, if expectations are high, or if you're unsure you have the skills required, you may find it hard to start the work. The solution? Face the fact that risk is inherent in everything you attempt. Recognize that failure is a valuable learning experience if you make it so. Winston Churchill said he would rather fail many times attempting the truly important than succeed at the trivial. When a task seems large and overwhelming, break it into smaller parts and set checkpoint deadlines for each.

Another reason for procrastination is **perfectionism.** You think you need more information, more material, more time to think, until you have procrastinated yourself into *paralysis by analysis.* This indecision will leave you less time to correct mistakes and will make it harder for you to meet deadlines. To conquer perfectionism, *just start*. How do you just start? By establishing a starting time as well as a completion deadline.

Boredom with unchallenging **work** is a third cause of procrastination. By putting off what we don't like to do, we end up doing it when our energy is lowest. Ironically, we then have to spend more time at it. To overcome boredom, set a starting time and write down a reward you enjoy but will not allow yourself to have until you have actually finished the boring task.

Finally, the feeling that you work best under **pressure** is a particularly destructive cause of procrastination. In the frantic atmosphere of a last-ditch effort, you create great stress for yourself and for others, increase the chances for mistakes, and leave no time to correct what goes wrong. So you almost always produce a product inferior to what you could have created at a realistic pace that allows time to review the work and to correct errors.

Leaving Tasks Unfinished

Closely related to Shifting Priorities, this timewaster occurs when your daily plan showing your Number One Priority is not in front of you. If you don't know your Number One Priority, leaving tasks unfinished becomes the story of your life. So, start with your first and take all possible action on tasks related to it before stopping. Then reward yourself with the knowledge that you've just furthered your first goal.

Lack of Delegation

Although you may not believe it, you're *not* the only one who can do a task well. If you insist on doing all important tasks yourself, many won't get done. Participants in seminars on time management are asked frequently how many tasks could be handled by someone else. The average answer is five. In reality, there are probably dozens. So, lack of delegation clearly ranks as a top timewaster.

Delegation is also a powerful training tool. Time invested in teaching another person how to do a task right saves you time over and over in the future. Remember, delegation is not used by just managers but by every professional.

To delegate effectively, follow these principles:

1. **Invest the time to become clear about the results you want.** Then, write them down. Don't subject a subordinate to shifting expectations because you were never sure what you wanted in the beginning. Even when the desired results are complex and sophisticated, describe them on paper. This will help you make them clear in your mind. You will be more effective in communicating them to the person to whom you are delegating.

2. **Think of desired results as goals.** Review the characteristics of effective goals in Chapter Two on pages 23-24. Make sure expected results are demanding, achievable, measurable, deadlined, written, and flexible. Then, communicate the expected results in terms that convey these qualities.

3. **Don't forget "owned by those affected."** When you're able to emphasize *results* rather than *method* in delegating, you allow the other person the satisfaction of contributing his or her ideas. You also save more of your time while delegating and during follow-up.

4. **Use common sense.** If the person wants or needs advice on method, provide it. But the more you are able to emphasize results over method, the more you will help the other person learn and develop a sense of confidence. And you will save more time in the long run!

5. **Ask the other person to summarize what you have discussed to check for understanding.** Ask for questions.

6. **Establish mutually agreed-upon procedures and checkpoints for evaluating progress.** When you do, you will be able to evaluate your progress quickly and efficiently.

7. **Accept risk as inherent.** Avoid perfectionism. Limit standards to what is acceptable. When you accept the fact that there will be a learning curve, you lay the groundwork for a much better payoff on your investment in the future.

Take a Moment...

Examine your goals for the next week. List below those tasks you will delegate. To whom will you delegate them? With what instructions? With what deadlines?

_____

_____

_____

_____

_____

_____

_____

_____

Inability to Say, "No"

There are many reasons people don't say, "No," when they should. They may have a desire to please, to help, to win approval, or to feel needed or important. They may fear offending someone. They may have lost sight of their own priorities. They may not know how. Saying, "No," doesn't have to sound impolite or unprofessional. Here are four steps which work well.

1. Listen. Give the person making the request your full attention. Make sure you fully understand what is being asked of you.

2. Say, "No." Be polite but firm. Don't build false hopes.

3. Give reasons. If appropriate, briefly explain your reasons.

4. Offer alternatives. Suggest other ways to meet the person's need.

Take a Moment...

Identify three times recently when you said, "Yes," and you should have said, "No." Using the four steps above, briefly rewrite the situations the way they should have gone.

1. _____

_____

2. _____

_____

3. _____

_____

Socializing

Socializing can eat up numerous hours of valuable time. Here are some ways to avoid the socializing time trap.

1. **Improve your ability to distinguish between keeping lines of communication open and needless socialization.** Evaluate other ways of obtaining necessary information on a regular basis. Have lunch. Use regularly scheduled breaks. Schedule focused meetings with targeted goals and agendas. Ask for periodic written updates.

2. **Recognize the urge to socialize.** Channel it to appropriate times so that it does not prevent you from achieving your Number One Priority. Be thoughtful of the time of others. It's their most valuable resource — and yours, too. You wouldn't think of squandering your own or someone else's money. Don't do it with time. When you're tempted to indulge in idle conversation and you haven't completed your Number One Priority, remind yourself, "Time is money." Then add, "Time is *more valuable* than money."

3. **Don't be flattered by an unnecessary social conversation.** Decide if it's more important than achieving your Number One Priority.

4. **Be candid.** State your deadline. Develop a repertoire of courteous, candid closings to conversations and become a master at using them as time management tools in friendly, straightforward ways. Few people really wish to corner someone into socializing when they know that person needs to get work done. It's counterproductive to relationships and, therefore, to communication down the road.

5. **Close your door.** If that doesn't work, find a hideaway.

4

6. When you've applied these solutions and have accomplished the priorities on your written daily plan, **leave your job at work.** Go socialize. You've earned it, so enjoy it! And then you won't be as tempted tomorrow to replace your Number One Priority with socializing.

Take a Moment...

List several courteous, candid closings to conversations — closings you would be comfortable using. During the next week, when you're tempted to socialize, use one of them and return to your Number One Priority. Record the results here. Practice and refine this time management tool until you become a master at it. Remember, you're really learning to manage yourself.

_____

_____

_____

_____

_____

_____

3 Lack of Control over the Work Environment

Elements in your work environment can be real timewasters. Here are some hints on how to deal with a few of the major timewasters.

Telephone

One of the most efficient tools for saving time, the telephone, also is a time management disaster. When we assume that a phone call is a legitimate demand for our attention and interrupt our own work to answer it, we are concluding that whatever the caller wants is more important than whatever we are doing. This is not always true. Remember your Number One Priority!

Beware of the following telephone traps:

- A desire to know what's happening.
- A handy excuse to leave a difficult or boring task.
- The urge to socialize before and after the business part of the call.
- A feeling of importance because others called you.
- Fear of offending.

Controlling the Telephone

Your telephone is a tool. It does not have a life of its own. Here are some of the best ways to control your phone time.

1. If possible, have an assistant, a machine, or voice mail screen your calls.

2. Return calls during a block of time convenient for you.

3. For each phone call you make, be prepared with notes, come to the point, and reach an understanding with the other person as to what action will be taken and when.

4. As soon as your business is finished, thank the other person and say good-bye courteously.

Drop-In Visitors

"Have you got a minute?" We all know this question never means *one* minute. It seldom means five, or even ten minutes. It really translates into "Can I interrupt your Number One Priority by coming in to talk?" But, most of us continue to permit drop-in visitors to infringe on our time.

To eliminate this timewaster, you must recognize and accept that drop-in visitors fritter away precious minutes that should be invested in achieving your Number One Priority. These minutes add up to years thrown away and goals not achieved. You must be motivated to handle drop-in visitors. Once you are, there are some specific techniques you can use:

1. **Greet the visitor**, explain briefly that you are working toward a deadline, and make an appointment for a more convenient time.

2. **Set a time limit at the beginning.** For example, "I have to leave in 15 minutes. Can we finish in that time?"

3. **Stand up when the visitor walks in** and remain standing during the conversation. Walk toward the door with the visitor as you acknowledge and summarize the conversation.

4. **Go to the other person's office**, where you are in control of when you leave: "I need ten minutes to wrap up this article. Why don't I come down to your office then?"

5. **Close your door**, and if possible, have an assistant screen your visitors.

Take a Moment...

How successful are you at managing interruptions? Take the following quiz to find out. If your total is below **15**, try some of the hints listed in the quiz and retake it again in three months.

Almost Never	= 0
Sometimes	= 1
Half the Time	= 2
Usually	= 3
Almost Always	= 4

1. Whenever possible, I complete tasks before permitting an interruption._____

2. Before accepting an interruption, I ask what it's about so I can assess its priority compared to my own._____

3. Before allowing an interruption, I explore alternatives: Is someone else better able to help? Can the interrupter solve the problem? Will postponing the action be better? _____

4. I use the telephone techniques suggested effectively. _____

5. With visitors, I use the techniques suggested effectively. _____

Total: _____

4

Meetings

The average manager spends ten hours a week in meetings, and 90 percent of managers say half that time is wasted. That's five hours a week, 250 hours a year — or six weeks — *for each person in the meeting*. If your organization holds meetings that rank high in frequency, but low in quality, here are some solutions:

1. **Invite only those people needed to solve the problem** — no more, no fewer.

2. **If the meeting does not apply to you, explain this to your boss.** Ask if you should attend the meeting or continue working on his or her Number One Priority.

3. **Prepare or request an agenda with time limits and written goals** for each topic. Make sure the agenda is circulated in advance. Work to keep the meeting focused on the agenda. Courteous reminders can help. For example, "Will we be able to deal with that before our time runs out today?" And, "That's a good point. If we don't get to it after we've covered the agenda items, drop me a note about it." Or, "If we don't take care of it independently, we can put it on next week's agenda."

4. **Decide the next steps.** As the last point for each item on the agenda, agree on the next action to be taken — who, how, and when.

5. **Start on time. End on time.**

6. **Prepare and circulate minutes.** Thorough follow-up depends on a good record of what action steps will be taken and by whom.

7. **Before you schedule a meeting, ask yourself if a memo or telephone call can accomplish what you need.**

Take a Moment...

Which meetings could be made more effective by using the preceding principles? List specific ways you will try to encourage use of these principles, even if you are not the person in charge of the meetings.

_____

_____

_____

Waiting and Travel Time

Consider that waiting or travel time is a golden opportunity. It is free of telephone and other office interruptions. Bring with you work that can be done in an airport or a waiting room. Plan the tasks you want to accomplish during longer travel time. Check off the tasks as you complete them, and reward yourself!

Untrained, Inadequate Staff

Recognize that untrained or inadequate staff hampers your ability to delegate. Lack of training or skill means you are not getting full value for your investment in staff. To correct the situation, take these steps:

1. **Assess the needs of the organization and of the trainees.**
2. **Design training which clearly addresses those needs** and which targets measurable goals.
3. **During implementation, support the training to signal that it is a high priority.** You may want to be involved in training two levels down to facilitate better selection of future team replacements.

> 66 **Authority is the power to do or get done the tasks for which you are responsible.** 99

4. **Measure the results.** Assess changed behavior, attitudes, and effectiveness at intervals after the training program. Follow up with evaluation and supplemental training to communicate that you are serious about developing an effective staff.

5. **Evaluate real staff needs and staff selection procedures.** Conduct training in these areas. If more staff is needed and finances are unavailable, assess your priorities again to make sure the most important ones get done.

6. **Evaluate staff time management practices.** Conduct training in this area. Implement a time management program targeted to save two hours per day per staff member. Have each staff member develop a written plan proposing what he or she would like to achieve in the two hours saved.

7. **Set regular times to measure the results of the above steps**, then reevaluate and follow up.

8. **Make full and effective use of your staff.** *Do nothing you can delegate.*

Confused Responsibility or Authority

When there is confusion about who is responsible for what, or a mismatch between responsibility and authority, much time and effort are wasted. Here are some common causes of this timewaster:

- Two people think they're each supposed to do a task, so it gets done twice.
- Two people think the other person is supposed to do a task, so it doesn't get done at all.
- One person has been given a task, but the other person doesn't know it and cannot cooperate.
- Two people think they each have been given the authority to do something and give conflicting instructions to others.

The solutions to this timewaster are **communication** and **clarification.**

1. If your job description is vague or nonexistent, you do not have to continue in this inefficient mode. Take charge of your own job. Draft a list of responsibilities or a full job description. If there is a potential overlap with another employee, identify the areas of duplication and try to resolve them.

2. When you are given responsibility for something, **clarify** that you also have been given the authority you need. Responsibility is the duty to do certain tasks or to see that they are performed. Authority is the power to do or get done the tasks for which you are responsible. For example, you may be responsible for supplies, but do you have the power to sign purchase orders for the necessary supplies? **Communication** needs to occur — preferably from your manager — if other team members are not aware of what authority you have been given to carry out an assigned responsibility.

The classic problem arises when you have been given a task to perform involving others who know nothing about your assignment. This problem can be solved at its inception by simply asking the person giving you the assignment if others who will be affected will be informed.

Take a Moment...

Describe the most recent time you experienced or observed overlapping or confused responsibility or authority. What were the outcomes in terms of total time invested, time wasted, and the quality of the results? What can be done to improve the outcomes in the future?

_____

_____

_____

_____

Lack of Standards, Controls, and Progress Reports

Choosing goals will do you no good if you do not develop an effective system to check progress and to ensure their completion. Whether you do so on paper or on a computer, it is crucial that you list your goals, the projects and steps needed to complete them, the planned date to start, the dates for progress checkpoints, and the deadline dates to finish. Then, use this progress report. It helps you achieve control over your goals and your time. Remember, anything which prevents you from achieving your goals is a timewaster. Without clear standards and a system of controls and progress reports, you cannot ensure that you will achieve your goals.

Unclear Communication

Clear communication is vital to efficient time management. Before you communicate anything, note your goal. State the goal clearly to the person with whom you are communicating, ask for input, agree on specific steps to achieve the goal, ask questions to check for understanding, and follow up to check performance, clarifying the communication as necessary. These steps are especially important for achieving effective delegation but can improve any communication.

Avoiding timewasters is essential to effective time management. Periodically, review the solutions for timewasters and keep them in mind as you work. If you do, you can save hundreds of hours each year.

Chapter Four Review

Please complete the following questions. Answers appear on page 93.

1. What are the two major definitions of a timewaster?

   _____

   _____

2. List the three major categories of timewasters.

   _____

   _____

   _____

3. What is the difference between the urgent and the important?

   _____

   _____

4. Concentrating your efforts on the critical _____ percent of your tasks will produce _____ percent of your results. That's why it's so important to _____.

4

CHAPTER FIVE

Your Personal Action Plan

Chapter Objectives:

After you have read this chapter and have completed the interactive exercises, you should be able to:

☑ Develop personal solutions for your timewasters.

☑ Develop your Personal Action Plan—with deadlines to ensure and measure your progress.

A timewaster occurs when your attention shift from one task to another is not worth it. Often it is a shift from a high-priority task to a low-priority task. In almost every case, the attention shift decreases both efficiency and effectiveness.

The problem is not just the time that the interruption takes, but the time you need to mentally catch up. Surveys show that it takes three times as long to recover from an interruption as it does to endure it. Sustained, focused attention creates the most efficient, effective results.

Eliminating Timewasters—Internal Review

The first step in eliminating timewasters was to research your own patterns of time use by filling in a Time Log.

You carried out the second step when you analyzed your Time Log.

The third step was to understand the major timewasters and their solutions.

You now are ready to identify your **top three personal timewasters.**

1. Look at the first attention shift recorded on your Time Log for day one.

2. If that attention shift seems to fit more than one timewaster, decide which timewaster reflects most accurately what was happening at the time your attention shifted.

3. Look at the next two pages for the Identifying Your Top Personal Timewasters sheet. In the blank beside that timewaster, record the number of minutes which elapsed before the next attention shift *or* before you returned to your Number One Priority.

   When a timewaster occurs more than once, use commas to separate the duration of each attention shift as follows: 1, 5, 3, 27.

4. Moving consecutively through the hours of the Time Log for day one, record the length of each interruption in minutes. Do the same for each day you took the Time Log.

5

IDENTIFYING YOUR TOP PERSONAL TIMEWASTERS

	Each interruption by this timewaster expressed in minutes	Total minutes used by this timewaster

Lack of Planning

Lack of goals/Unclear objectives	_____	_____
Lack of daily priorities	_____	_____
Shifting priorities	_____	_____
Crisis management	_____	_____
Attempting too much	_____	_____
Unrealistic time estimates	_____	_____

Lack of Self-Management

Lack of self-discipline	_____	_____
Personal disorganization	_____	_____
Cluttered desk	_____	_____
Inadequate filing system	_____	_____
Paperwork	_____	_____

IDENTIFYING YOUR TOP PERSONAL TIMEWASTERS

	Each interruption by this timewaster expressed in minutes	Total minutes used by this timewaster

Lack of Self-Management (Continued)

Procrastination _____ _____

Paralysis by analysis _____ _____

Leaving tasks unfinished _____ _____

Lack of delegation _____ _____

Inability to say, "No" _____ _____

Socializing _____ _____

Lack of Control over the Work Environment

Telephone _____ _____

Drop-In Visitors _____ _____

Meetings _____ _____

Waiting time and travel time _____ _____

Untrained, inadequate staff _____ _____

Confused authority and responsibility _____ _____

Lack of standards, controls, and progress reports _____ _____

Unclear communication _____ _____

Completing the Personal Action Plan—Identifying Causes and Selecting Solutions

Using the Personal Action Plan for Eliminating Timewasters on pages 80-81, list the name of the timewaster next to "1." which used the greatest total number of minutes throughout the period of your Time Log. Next, list the timewaster which took the second greatest number of total minutes. Continue doing this until you have listed your top fifteen timewasters, in descending order by the total number of minutes wasted.

66 By eliminating your top three timewasters, you should recover two hours a day to invest as you choose. 99

To Finish the Personal Action Plan, Complete the Following Steps:

1. Locate your top three timewasters in Chapter Four and identify the causes which apply to your situation.
2. Select the solutions most likely to be effective in your situation.
3. Enter this information, along with start dates and dates to check progress on the first three lines of your Personal Action Plan on pages 80-81.

For the first three weeks, concentrate on eliminating your top three timewasters. Success in replacing the top three with good habits will yield at least two hours a day for you to invest as you choose. If you understand the most important principle of time management, you will direct that recovered time toward your Number One Priority until you have accomplished it.

Next, list tentative start dates (three weeks from now) to begin eliminating timewasters 4, 5, and 6.

Continue the process, eliminating three more timewasters by the end of each three-week period. Continually monitor your progress to prevent backsliding on the timewasters already eliminated.

Be sure to post the Personal Action Plan close to your desk where you can see it.

At the end of 15 weeks, take another Time Log for three days. Describe the results below. Have you eliminated your top three timewasters? Your top six? Of your top 15 timewasters, which ones do you feel you have under control? Which are still giving you trouble? Why? Go back to Chapter Four and read the sections on the timewasters which are still giving you trouble. List the recommended solutions you will adopt.

_____

_____

_____

_____

Write the date by which you will have eliminated the rest of your top 15 timewasters.

_____

Enter this date on the Personal Action Plan posted near your desk.

At the end of 15 weeks (almost four months), assess the degree to which you have achieved your first priorities during that period. Analyze the progress you have made toward your written long-range goals. and describe the results here. After you've done that, complete another Personal Action Plan and post it. Don't delay.

_____

_____

_____

PERSONAL ACTION PLAN FOR

TIMEWASTER	CAUSE(S)	SOLUTION(S)
1.		
2.		
3.		
4.		
5.		
6.		
7.		
8.		
9.		
10.		
11.		
12.		
13.		
14.		
15.		

ELIMINATING TIMEWASTERS

Start Date	Check Date	Corrective Action Taken	Completion Date

5

CHAPTER SIX

Advanced Time Tactics—Putting It All Together

Chapter Objectives:

After you have read this chapter and have completed the interactive exercises, you should be able to:

- ☑ Understand the nature of habits.
- ☑ Know how to exchange bad habits for good ones.
- ☑ Understand the Quiet Hour and know how to use it.
- ☑ Understand your Personal Energy Cycle and know how to use it.
- ☑ Develop your ideal day.
- ☑ Internalize the Number-One Principle of Time Management.

In this book we have developed the basic principles of the *Time Tactics® Process*. They are:

- ■ Set goals.
- ■ Understand the major timewasters and their solutions.
- ■ Make the commitment to fill in a Time Log .
- ■ Identify your top personal timewasters.
- ■ Develop your Personal Action Plan.
    - √ Eliminate your top timewasters.
    - √ Plot your Personal Energy Cycle.
    - √ Develop your ideal day.
- ■ Plan each day before you start it.
- ■ Identify your Number One Priority and get it done first.

You also have learned to apply the concepts of **commitment**, **choice**, and **control** throughout the *Time Tactics® Process*.

In this chapter, we will explore some additional tools which are exceptionally helpful in implementing the total *Time Tactics® Process*. These tools include effective techniques for changing habits, such as the Quiet Hour, the Personal Energy Cycle, and the Ideal Day.

The Nature of Habits

Habits are amazing. Few of us could explain why we do certain things the way we do. Right now, you are trying to eliminate your top three timewasters and, if you haven't already, you will soon come face to face with the hard fact that unlearning old habits that don't work well is difficult but essential. Fortunately, there is an established process for teaching ourselves new habits, and it works:

The philosopher William James developed this highly successful method for replacing bad habits with good ones. He said that one should:

- Clearly state the desired goal.
- Recognize the difficulty of changing.
- Launch the new habit strongly.
- Practice the new habit often.
- Do not allow even one exception until the habit is firmly ingrained.

> 66 Consider the postage stamp: its usefulness consists in the ability to stick to one thing until it gets the job done. 99
>
> **Josh Billings**

The Quiet Hour

The Quiet Hour is one of the most successful and profitable time management techniques ever devised. For one hour a day, no phone calls, no visitors, no conversation, no interruptions of any kind — just quiet, uninterrupted work. If you don't have an assistant to field all calls and visitors, use your answering machine or voice mail and close your door.

Almost without exception, everyone who has tried a Quiet Hour supports the idea enthusiastically. The results? On average, a person gets done in one Quiet Hour what would take three "normal" interrupted hours. Talk about productivity improvement!

What's the best time for the Quiet Hour? First thing in the morning, before the tempo of calls and meetings is up to speed. The Quiet Hour works even better if all in the organization participate and all have their Quiet Hours at the same time.

Sometimes people decide that a few very important clients are a more important priority than a Quiet Hour that is never interrupted. Yet they don't want to keep their door open to everybody during this valuable hour. For example, in this age of seven-foot basketball players, one coach solved the problem of drop-in visitors with this sign: "This is my Quiet Hour. Don't come in unless you can see over the transom."

Take a Moment...

How will you use your Quiet Hour?

_____

_____

_____

Your Personal Energy Cycle

Most of us have certain times of the day when we're more energetic and mentally fresher. At other times, we're less effective. If we use our best working times to complete those tasks which are most important, most challenging, and require the most focus, our productivity increases dramatically. We get more done and the results are better.

But if we fritter away our best working time through procrastination or lack of planning, we leave important, challenging tasks for the time when our energy and mental alertness has run down. This means everything takes longer and isn't done as well. More mistakes are made. Even more time is needed to correct them. Clearly, the investment of time is not yielding maximum return.

If you make a habit of scheduling key tasks during your peak energy levels, you can easily double your productivity in both quantity and quality. Please reread both your Time Log and the Analysis of Your Time Log, which begins on page 41, for clues to help you complete the following chart and answer the following questions:

Rate your typical energy level for each hour in your day. Use 5 for the highest energy, 0 for the lowest.

5:00 AM	_____
6:00 AM	_____
7:00 AM	_____
8:00 AM	_____
9:00 AM	_____
10:00 AM	_____
11:00 AM	_____
12:00 PM	_____
1:00 PM	_____
2:00 PM	_____

6

3:00 PM	_____
4:00 PM	_____
5:00 PM	_____
6:00 PM	_____
7:00 PM	_____
8:00 PM	_____
9:00 PM	_____
10:00 PM	_____
11:00 PM	_____

Are you a slow starter or do you do your best work in the morning?

_____

If not first thing in the morning, when do you do your best work?

_____

Do you have an energy dip after lunch?

_____

Mid-afternoon? _____ If not, when? _____

Do you get a second wind around 4:00 PM?

_____

Do you have a regular exercise time?

_____

What short-term and long-term effects does exercise have on your energy cycle? That is, if you exercise early in the morning, does it energize you? Or does it leave you tired from missing an hour of sleep?

_____

List the hours when you typically have the most focused concentration and energy.

_____

What specific things are you usually doing in your most energetic hours?

_____

What specific activities will you do during your best hours, starting today?

_____

List the hours when you typically have the lowest energy and concentration.

_____

Control Over Your Day and Your Destiny: Developing Your Ideal Day

The Ideal Day you will develop next is a powerful tool for implementing your personal time management program. You can plan your Ideal Day around your Personal Energy Cycle and use it to schedule your key tasks for your best working times. Your goal will be to work on those tasks at the same time each day.

You may think that your job is filled with so many unique projects, unusual problems, crises, and interruptions that you have no such thing as a "typical" day. As one manager put it, "The only thing typical about my days is their diversity." Yet, all of us have significant tasks that occur more or less regularly. Who decides when you do these things, at what hour of the day? You do. For best time management you need to make those decisions so they create an Ideal Day.

❝ Matching your task demands to your energy cycle can double your productivity. ❞

6

Your Ideal Day will become a model for each Daily Plan you develop in the future. Your Ideal Day will be different from someone else's because it is based on your Personal Energy Cycle. It will indicate blocks of time for your major categories of tasks. Then, for each Daily Plan, you will schedule the specifics in each major category.

Categories might include Number One Priority, Number Two Priority, Number Three Priority, Checkpoints on Projects, Appointments, Meetings, Phone Calls, Call Backs, To-Do List (for lower-priority items, if you get to them), Exercise, Family Time, Personal Time. You design the categories and the placement of the blocks of time during which they will be carried out. Then add, subtract, and transform them until they best suit your personal and professional life.

List your categories below:

_____

_____

_____

_____

Next, examine the Sample Daily Plan on the next page. Then, block out your Ideal Day on the blank Daily Plan on page 90.

When you have completed your Ideal Day, develop your Daily Plan for the next five days. Your thinking process should follow this sequence:

1. **Start** with your long-range and interim goals.
2. **Choose** the tasks which will achieve those goals.
3. **Assign** priorities to the day's tasks, according to their long-range importance and their immediacy. Use the Priority Matrix you learned in Chapter Four.

4. **Schedule** tasks, according to the priority you have determined and the degree of concentration required.

5. **Use** the Daily Plan to control interruptions, to know what to do next, and, above all, to accomplish your top priorities. Remember, now that you have invested time in making the hard choices, your Daily Plan puts you in control. That's the payoff on your investment.

SAMPLE DAILY PLAN

FEBRUARY   *WEEK 8*   *19##*

Monday 17	Tuesday 18	Wednesday 19	Thursday 20	Friday 21	Saturday 22
Tasks	*Tasks*	*Tasks*	*Tasks*	*Tasks*	
1. Draft Video Costs	1. Slides	1. Review pkg. in house	1. Final Draft Video	1. Graphics	8:00 Sam—tennis
2. Staff Meeting	2. Back Correspond.	2. Sam's Proposal			
3. Newton Proposal		3. Final Draft			

Appointments	*Appointments*	*Appointments*	*Appointments*	*Appointments*	
8:00 am	*8:00 am*	*8:00 am*	*8:00 am*	*8:00 am*	
9:00 am	*9:00 am*	*9:00 am*	*9:00 am* no appts.	*9:00 am* no appts.	
Tom - Recruiting	Meet with Sue				
10:00 am	*10:00 am*	*10:00 am*	*10:00 am*	*10:00 am*	
	Staff Meeting				
11:00 am	*11:00 am*	*11:00 am*	*11:00 am*	*11:00 am*	1:00 Shopping - Lea
12:00 pm	*12:00 pm*	*12:00 pm*	*12:00 pm*	*12:00 pm*	
Nevins Eatery			Sam at Fox's		
1:00 pm	*1:00 pm*	*1:00 pm*	*1:00 pm*	*1:00 pm*	
	Review Videos				
2:00 pm	*2:00 pm*	*2:00 pm*	*2:00 pm*	*2:00 pm*	
		Mary - Printing		ck/Harry - Videos	
3:00 pm	*3:00 pm*	*3:00 pm*	*3:00 pm*	*3:00 pm*	
	Tom - Presentation		Review with Tom		
4:00 pm	*4:00 pm*	*4:00 pm*	*4:00 pm*	*4:00 pm*	
Agenda to Typing	Final Draft				
5:00 pm	*5:00 pm*	*5:00 pm*	*5:00 pm*	*5:00 pm*	Sunday 23
					Set VCR Ch. 13
6:00 pm	*6:00 pm*	*6:00 pm*	*6:00 pm*	*6:00 pm*	@ 10 pm
		Cocktails - Sims			
7:00 pm	*7:00 pm*	*7:00 pm*	*7:00 pm*	*7:00 pm*	

To Do:	*To Do:*	*To Do:*	*To Do:*	*To Do:*	
Jim - Editing	Call JB	Order Jerry's Cake	For lunch w/Sam,	Stop at store for Lea	
		Sims 555-1212	Figures on Proposal		
Read Jacobsen Article	Sam	12 Park - Eatery 8pm	Needs List		

89

DAILY PLAN

MONTH_____ WEEK _____ 19__

| Day/Date
Goals | Day/Date
Goals | Day/Date
Goals | Day/Date
Goals | Day/Date
Goals | Day/Date
Tasks |
|---|---|---|---|---|---|
| _____ | _____ | _____ | _____ | _____ | _____ |
| _____ | _____ | _____ | _____ | _____ | _____ |
| _____ | _____ | _____ | _____ | _____ | _____ |

| Appointments
8:00 am | Appointments
8:00 am | Appointments
8:00 am | Appointments
8:00 am | Appointments
8:00 am | Appointments
8:00 am |
|---|---|---|---|---|---|
| 9:00 am | 9:00 am | 9:00 am | 9:00 am | 9:00 am | 9:00 am |
| 10:00 am | 10:00 am | 10:00 am | 10:00 am | 10:00 am | 10:00 am |
| 11:00 am | 11:00 am | 11:00 am | 11:00 am | 11:00 am | 11:00 am |
| 12:00 pm | 12:00 pm | 12:00 pm | 12:00 pm | 12:00 pm | 12:00 pm |
| 1:00 pm | 1:00 pm | 1:00 pm | 1:00 pm | 1:00 pm | 1:00 pm |
| 2:00 pm | 2:00 pm | 2:00 pm | 2:00 pm | 2:00 pm | 2:00 pm |
| 3:00 pm | 3:00 pm | 3:00 pm | 3:00 pm | 3:00 pm | 3:00 pm |
| 4:00 pm | 4:00 pm | 4:00 pm | 4:00 pm | 4:00 pm | 4:00 pm |
| 5:00 pm | 5:00 pm | 5:00 pm | 5:00 pm | 5:00 pm | 5:00 pm |
| 6:00 pm | 6:00 pm | 6:00 pm | 6:00 pm | 6:00 pm | 6:00 pm |
| 7:00 pm | 7:00 pm | 7:00 pm | 7:00 pm | 7:00 pm | 7:00 pm |

To Do:	To Do:	To Do:	To Do:	To Do:	To Do:
_____	_____	_____	_____	_____	_____
_____	_____	_____	_____	_____	_____
_____	_____	_____	_____	_____	_____
_____	_____	_____	_____	_____	_____
_____	_____	_____	_____	_____	_____

In Conclusion

Now that you have been through all the stages of the *Time Tactics®
Process*, you are ready to hit the ground running. With all the time
management tools you have learned, your life will be changed forever.

Be alert for backsliding, but don't let it get you down. Use the philosophy
of learning from mistakes to continually improve your ability to manage
yourself and your time. Each day, evaluate your effectiveness in:

■ Making choices and establishing goals.

■ Planning your day.

■ Prioritizing.

■ Implementing your Personal Action Plan.

■ Carrying out a Daily Plan based on your Ideal Day.

■ Managing yourself and your time to achieve both career and
personal goals.

Remember: The virtue of time management is its simplicity.

> **Congratulations!
> You've chosen to be in control
> of yourself, your time, and your life!**

**" Remember to
keep both your
Daily Plan and
your Personal
Action Plan in
front of you
each day. "**

6

Answers to Chapter Reviews

Chapter One Review (page 19)

1. Change, goals, resource
2. Commitment, control
3. A) Wasting time causes stress
   B) Managing time improves productivity
   C) Managing time improves your quality of life
4. F
5. F
6. F

Chapter Two Review (page 33)

1. T
2. T
3. T
4. F

(Deadlined goals must be realistic, or they will not be met. They should be flexible enough to accommodate the unforeseen, making it more likely that the original deadline will be met and making it possible to finish before the deadline if the unforeseen does not occur. Finishing early also permits more time to inspect the product for imperfections.)

5. F

(Measuring progress toward goals is a great motivator and an effective way of detecting needed course correction.)

6.
Owned by those affected	Deadlined
Demanding	Written
Achievable	Flexible
Measurable	

7. Sustainability of the relationship between you and your organization and maximum achievement for both you and your organization.

Chapter Four Review (page 73)

1. A timewaster is:
   - Anything which decreases your productivity and your effectiveness.
   - Anything which causes a shift in attention away from your Number One Priority.
2. Lack of Planning, Lack of Self-Management, Lack of Control over the Work Environment
3. An urgent task is one that **must be done now,** whether it has little importance or great importance. A task with long-range importance is one that you could look back on at the end of a year and **know that it was vital** that you spent time on it.
4. Concentrating your efforts on the critical **20 percent** of your tasks will produce **80 percent** of your results. That's why it's so important to **prioritize.**

NOTES

NOTES

NOTES